SUPPLEMENTARY STUDIES
for Eb and BBb Basses

To be used with, or to follow any method.

R. M. ENDRESEN

Fingerings for Eb Bass

Fingerings for BBb Bass

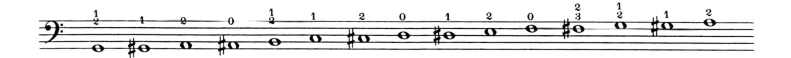

Copyright MCMXXXVI by Rubank Inc., Chicago, Ill.
International Copyright Secured

1

*The BBb fingering is indicated first, followed by the Eb fingering in parenthesis. When only one fingering is given it is for both.

3

Marziale

4

Allegro

3

5

Andante

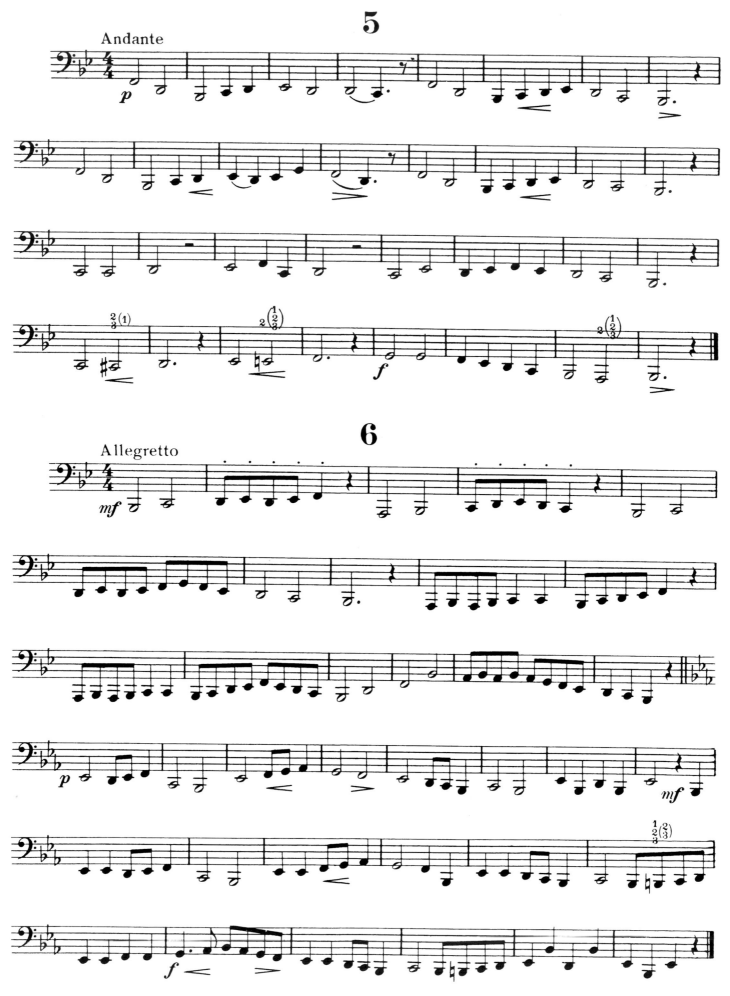

6

Allegretto

9

Moderato

10

March tempo

11

SCALE STUDY

12

13

Allegretto

14

Majestic

15

16

17

Moderato

18

Andante cantabile

19

20

21

SCALE STUDY

22

Moderato

25

26

27

Moderato

Misterioso

Allegretto

28

CHROMATIC STUDY

29

Moderato

30

Valse tempo

31

32

35

38

39

40

44

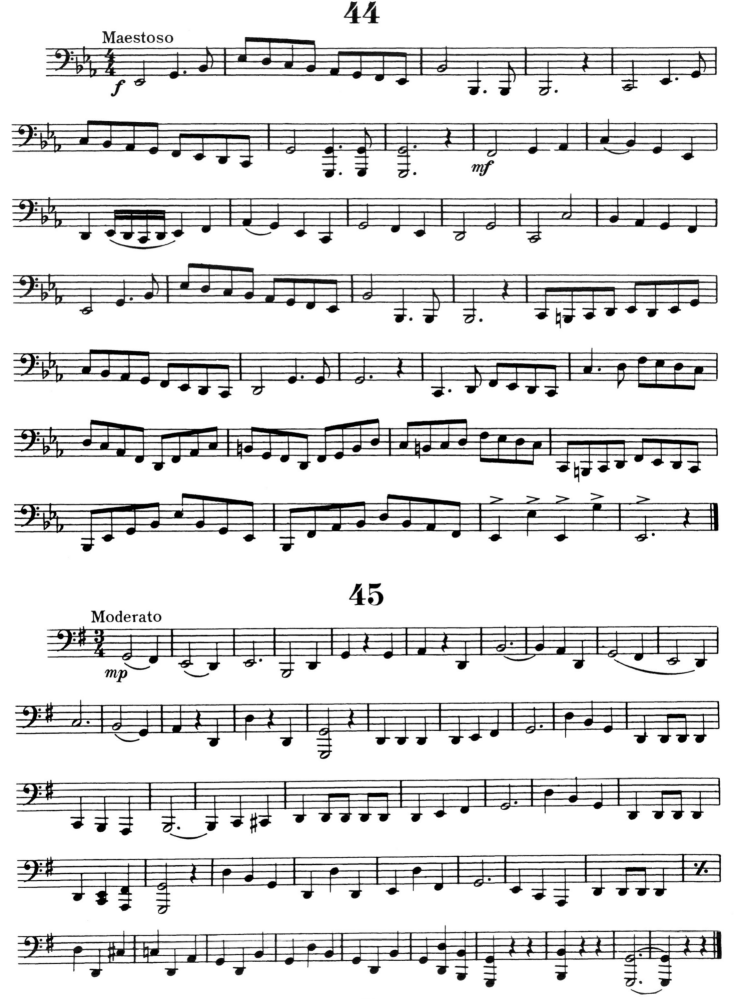

45